Sports and Activities

Let's Go Camping!

by Jan Mader

Consulting Editor: Gail Saunders-Smith, PhD

Consultant: Kymm Ballard, MA
Physical Education, Athletics, and Sports Medicine Consultant
North Carolina Department of Public Instruction

Capstone
press

Mankato, Minnesota

Pebble Plus is published by Capstone Press,
151 Good Counsel Drive, P.O. Box 669, Mankato, Minnesota 56002.
www.capstonepress.com

1 2 3 4 5 6 11 10 09 08 07 06

Library of Congress Cataloging-in-Publication Data
Mader, Jan.
    Let's go camping! / by Jan Mader.
    p. cm.—(Pebble plus. Sports and activities)
    Summary: "Simple text and photographs present the skills, equipment, and safety concerns
of camping"—Provided by publisher.
    Includes bibliographical references and index.
    ISBN-13: 978-0-7368-6360-5 (hardcover)
    ISBN-10: 0-7368-6360-5 (hardcover)
    1. Camping—Juvenile literature. I. Title. II. Series.
GV191.7.M264 2007
796.54—dc22   2006000499

Editorial Credits
Amber Bannerman, editor; Juliette Peters, set designer; Bobbi J. Wyss, book designer; Kelly Garvin,
    photo researcher/photo editor

Photo Credits
Capstone Press/Karon Dubke, 13, 14–15; TJ Thoraldson Digital Photography, cover, 1, 17
Corbis/Ariel Skelley, 6–7, 21; Layne Kennedy, 18–19
Getty Images Inc./David Vance, 5; Jan Von Holleben, 8–9; Michael Hart, 11

**Capstone Press would like to thank Dale and Marlene Eckstrom (pictured on page 17) of St. James,
    Minnesota, for the use of their camper for this book.**

Note to Parents and Teachers

The Sports and Activities set supports national physical education standards related
to recognizing movement forms and exhibiting a physically active lifestyle. This book
describes and illustrates camping. The images support early readers in understanding the
text. The repetition of words and phrases helps early readers learn new words. This book
also introduces early readers to subject-specific vocabulary words, which are defined in
the Glossary section. Early readers may need assistance to read some words and to use
the Table of Contents, Glossary, Read More, Internet Sites, and Index sections of the book.

Table of Contents

Going Camping

Fish, hike, swim, and sing!
Have fun camping with
family and friends.

People camp in tents,

motor homes, and cabins.

They set up their things

at a campsite.

Campers cook over campfires.

They roast hot dogs

with a stick.

Camping Equipment

Campers pack clothes
and hiking shoes.
They remember their
fishing pole and bait.

Flashlights help campers
see in the dark.

Sleeping bags keep campers
warm and cozy.
They fall asleep breathing
the fresh night air.

Camping Safety

Wild animals like camp food.
Campers put their food away
before leaving their campsite.

Campers pack a first aid kit.

They use bandages

for scrapes and cuts.

Having Fun

Marshmallows, graham
crackers, and chocolate.
Let's sit around the campfire
and make s'mores!

Glossary

cabin—a small house, often built of wood

camp—to live outdoors in a tent, a cabin, or a motor home for a period of time

campfire—a fire made at a campsite to cook food or to stay warm

hike—to take a long walk

motor home—a small house on wheels

sleeping bag—a large, warmly-lined bag used mainly for sleeping outdoors

s'mores—a dessert made from chocolate, graham crackers, and marshmallows

tent—a large piece of cloth held up by ropes and poles that is used for shelter

Read More

Ching, Jacqueline. *Camping: Have Fun, Be Smart.* Explore the Outdoors. New York: Rosen, 2000.

George, Kristine O'Connell. *Toasting Marshmallows: Camping Poems.* New York: Clarion Books, 2001.

Seeberg, Tim. *Camping.* Kids' Guides to the Outdoors. Chanhassen, Minn.: Child's World, 2004.

Internet Sites

FactHound offers a safe, fun way to find Internet sites related to this book. All of the sites on FactHound have been researched by our staff.

Here's how:

1. Visit *www.facthound.com*

2. Choose your grade level.

3. Type in this book ID **0736863605** for age-appropriate sites. You may also browse subjects by clicking on letters, or by clicking on pictures and words.

4. Click on the **Fetch It** button.

FactHound will fetch the best sites for you!

Index

Word Count: 114
Grade: 1
Early-Intervention Level: 14